INSTAGRAM MARKETING SIMPLIFIED

"Strategies, Tips, and Tactics for Effortless Social Media Success"

VINCENT SIMS

Copyright ©

Dedication

"This book is dedicated to every entrepreneur, marketer, and dreamer seeking clarity in the dynamic realm of Instagram marketing. May these simplified strategies pave the way for your success in navigating the ever-evolving landscape of social media. Here's to simplifying the journey and amplifying your presence!"

Table of Contents

Acknowledgments

"I would like to express my sincere gratitude to the Instagram community for its continuous inspiration and innovation. Special thanks to the tireless marketers, creators, and entrepreneurs who generously shared their insights, contributing to the wealth of knowledge in this book. My appreciation extends to my supportive network, friends, and family, whose encouragement fueled the creation of 'Instagram Marketing Simplified.' Your support has been invaluable on this journey to demystify and simplify the art of Instagram marketing."

Preface

"In an age dominated by social media, mastering the art of Instagram marketing has become imperative for businesses and individuals alike. 'Instagram Marketing Simplified' is born out of a passion to demystify the complexities surrounding this powerful platform. This book aims to distill the vast realm of Instagram marketing into clear, actionable strategies for beginners and seasoned professionals alike.

As you embark on this journey, you'll find practical insights, real-world examples, and simplified techniques that cut through the noise of social media marketing. Whether you're looking to boost brand awareness, engage with your audience, or drive conversions, this book is crafted to empower you with the knowledge and confidence needed to navigate the dynamic landscape of Instagram.

By simplifying the intricacies of Instagram marketing, we hope to unlock the full potential of your online presence. Let the pages ahead guide you through the essentials, and may this resource be a catalyst for your success in the vibrant world of social media. Happy marketing!"

Chapter 1.

Introduction to Instagram Marketing

- Understanding the Power of Instagram

Welcome to the dynamic world of Instagram Marketing, where visual storytelling meets strategic promotion, creating a powerful blend that can transform your online presence. In this digital age, Instagram has emerged as one of the most influential platforms, offering unparalleled opportunities for businesses, brands, and individuals to connect with their audience on a global scale.

Understanding the Power of Instagram:

Instagram's impact goes beyond just being a photo-sharing app; it has evolved into a vibrant ecosystem that thrives on creativity, engagement, and community. With over a billion monthly active users, Instagram has become a powerhouse for marketing, enabling businesses to showcase their products, services, and stories in compelling visual formats.

Visual Appeal:
One of Instagram's defining features is its emphasis on visuals. Whether it's eye-catching images, captivating videos, or engaging stories, the platform is designed to capture attention instantly. Understanding the visual appeal of Instagram is crucial for crafting content that not only stands out but also resonates with your target audience.

Engagement and Connection:
Instagram is not just a broadcasting channel; it's a two-way street that fosters engagement and connection. Features like

comments, likes, direct messages, and interactive elements such as polls and quizzes make it easier than ever to build a community around your brand. The power lies in creating content that sparks conversations, elicits emotions, and encourages participation.

Influencer Culture:
The rise of influencers has significantly contributed to the power dynamics on Instagram. Collaborating with influencers who align with your brand values can amplify your reach and credibility. Understanding the nuances of influencer marketing on Instagram opens doors to new audiences and builds trust through authentic recommendations.

Algorithmic Insights:
Navigating Instagram's algorithm is a key aspect of unlocking its marketing potential. From understanding the relevance of hashtags to optimizing posting times and

leveraging the Explore page, grasping the intricacies of the algorithm is essential for maximizing your content's visibility.

Business Tools and Analytics:
Instagram provides a suite of business tools and analytics that empowers marketers to track performance, understand audience demographics, and refine strategies. Utilizing these insights allows for data-driven decisions, ensuring that your marketing efforts are aligned with your goals and resonating with your audience.

As we delve deeper into the realm of Instagram Marketing, each chapter will unravel strategies, tips, and techniques to simplify your approach, helping you harness the full power of this dynamic platform. Get ready to embark on a journey where creativity meets strategy, and your brand's story takes center stage in the captivating world of Instagram.

- Key Benefits for Businesses

In the ever-evolving landscape of digital marketing, Instagram stands out as a powerhouse, offering a plethora of benefits for businesses looking to enhance their online presence, engage with their audience, and drive meaningful results. Let's explore the key advantages that make Instagram an indispensable tool for businesses.

1. Global Reach and Visibility:
   Instagram's massive user base of over a billion people provides businesses with unparalleled global reach. By strategically leveraging hashtags, location tags, and shareable content, businesses can extend their visibility to audiences around the world.

2. Visual Storytelling:

Instagram's emphasis on visual content allows businesses to tell their stories more compellingly and engagingly. Through high-quality images and videos, brands can showcase their products, services, and values, fostering a deeper connection with their audience.

3. Community Building:

Instagram's interactive features, such as comments, likes, and direct messages, facilitate direct communication with followers. Building a community around your brand fosters loyalty and creates a sense of belonging, turning followers into loyal customers and advocates.

4. Influencer Collaborations:

Partnering with influencers who align with your brand can significantly amplify your reach and credibility. Influencer collaborations provide authentic endorsements, reaching new audiences and building trust through the influencer's established rapport with their followers.

5. E-commerce Integration:
Instagram has evolved into a powerful e-commerce platform with features like shoppable posts and the Instagram Shop. Businesses can seamlessly integrate their products into the platform, providing a frictionless shopping experience for users.

6. Targeted Advertising:
Instagram's parent company, Facebook, offers robust advertising tools that allow businesses to create highly targeted ad campaigns. From demographics to interests, businesses can tailor their ads to reach specific audience segments, maximizing the effectiveness of their marketing budget.

7. Storytelling with Instagram Stories:
Instagram Stories offer a dynamic way for businesses to share time-sensitive content,

behind-the-scenes glimpses, and limited-time promotions. The ephemeral nature of Stories encourages daily engagement and keeps followers consistently interested in your brand.

8. Analytics and Insights:

Instagram's business tools provide detailed analytics, offering insights into audience demographics, engagement metrics, and the performance of individual posts. Businesses can use this data to refine their strategies, ensuring they are resonating with their target audience.

9. Hashtag Campaigns:

Strategic use of hashtags can amplify the reach of your content and create a sense of community around specific campaigns. Hashtag campaigns encourage user participation, driving organic engagement and user-generated content.

10. Constant Innovation:

Instagram continues to evolve by introducing new features and tools. Staying abreast of these innovations allows businesses to adapt their strategies, ensuring they remain at the forefront of the platform's capabilities.

As businesses navigate the competitive landscape, integrating Instagram into their marketing toolkit can be a game-changer, offering a unique combination of visual appeal, community engagement, and strategic advertising. The benefits outlined here are just the tip of the iceberg, and with a thoughtful approach, businesses can unlock the full potential of Instagram for sustainable growth and success.

- Overview of Instagram Marketing Landscape

The Instagram marketing landscape is a dynamic terrain where creativity, strategy, and engagement converge to form a powerful platform for businesses and individuals alike. Understanding the key elements of this landscape is essential for crafting effective marketing strategies and capitalizing on the myriad opportunities it presents.

1. Visual-Centric Platform:
   At the core of Instagram's allure is its emphasis on visual content. From striking images to engaging videos, the platform encourages users to share their stories in a visually compelling manner. This focus on aesthetics has transformed Instagram into a hub for creativity, making it an ideal space for brands to showcase their personality and products.

2. Diverse Content Formats:

Instagram offers a variety of content formats to cater to different preferences. Feed posts, Instagram Stories, IGTV, and Reels provide businesses with versatile tools to connect with their audience. Adapting content to suit these formats enables brands to diversify their approach and keep their audience engaged across various touchpoints.

3. Engagement and Interactivity:

Instagram thrives on engagement, offering features like likes, comments, direct messages, and polls. Successful marketing on Instagram involves fostering two-way communication with the audience. Responding to comments, encouraging participation, and leveraging interactive elements contribute to a vibrant and engaged community.

4. Algorithmic Dynamics:

Understanding Instagram's algorithm is crucial for optimizing content visibility. The algorithm considers factors like user interactions, post-recency, and relevance to determine what appears on a user's feed. Marketers need to be strategic in utilizing hashtags, posting at optimal times, and creating engaging content to navigate the algorithm effectively.

5. Influencer Marketing Influence:
The rise of influencers has reshaped the marketing landscape on Instagram. Collaborating with influencers allows brands to tap into established audiences, build credibility, and gain exposure. Identifying the right influencers whose values align with the brand's message is pivotal for successful influencer partnerships.

6. Instagram Ads Platform:
Instagram's advertising platform offers businesses a targeted and measurable way to reach their audience. Whether through

sponsored posts, Stories ads, or carousel ads, businesses can leverage these tools to amplify their reach and drive specific objectives, such as website visits or app installations.

7. Hashtags as Discoverability Tools:

Hashtags play a significant role in enhancing discoverability on Instagram. Strategic use of relevant hashtags increases the visibility of posts and connects content with users interested in specific topics. Crafting branded hashtags and participating in trending conversations contribute to a broader reach.

8. Analytics and Insights:

Instagram provides robust analytics tools for business accounts, offering valuable insights into audience demographics, post-performance, and engagement metrics. Analyzing these data points allows marketers to refine their strategies, tailoring content to better resonate with their target audience.

9. E-commerce Integration:

With the introduction of features like shoppable posts and Instagram Shop, the platform has evolved into an e-commerce destination. Businesses can seamlessly integrate their products, creating a streamlined shopping experience for users without leaving the app.

10. Constant Evolution:

Instagram is known for its commitment to innovation. Regular updates and the introduction of new features ensure that the platform remains relevant and adaptive to changing trends. Staying informed about these updates enables marketers to leverage the latest tools for maximum impact.

In this ever-evolving landscape, mastering Instagram marketing involves a blend of creativity, adaptability, and strategic thinking. As we delve deeper into specific strategies and tactics, this overview serves as a foundation for navigating the intricacies of Instagram and harnessing its vast potential for marketing success.

Chapter 2.

Setting Up Your Instagram Business Profile

- Creating a Compelling Bio

Your Instagram bio is the gateway to your brand's world on the platform—a concise and powerful introduction that can captivate your audience and convey the essence of your business. Follow these steps to create a compelling bio that leaves a lasting impression.

1. Concise Introduction:

Begin with a clear and concise introduction. State who you are or what your business is about in a few words.

Use language that resonates with your target audience and reflects your brand's personality.

2. Showcase Your Unique Selling Proposition (USP):

Highlight what sets your business apart. Whether it's a unique product, outstanding service, or a compelling mission, communicate your USP succinctly. This is your opportunity to grab attention and differentiate yourself in a crowded digital space.

3. Contact Information:

Include essential contact information such as email addresses, phone numbers, or a link to your website. Making it easy for potential customers to get in touch or explore more about your offerings enhances accessibility and trust.

4. Relevant Keywords and Hashtags:

Integrate relevant keywords and hashtags related to your industry or niche. This improves the discoverability of your profile when users search for specific topics. Think about the terms your audience might use when looking for businesses like yours.

5. Embrace Emojis:
Emojis can add a playful and visually appealing touch to your bio. Use them strategically to complement your message or highlight key points. However, avoid overusing emojis to maintain a professional tone.

6. Call-to-Action (CTA):
Encourage your audience to take a specific action. Whether it's visiting your website, exploring your latest products, or participating in a campaign, a clear CTA guides your followers on the next steps you want them to take.

7. Story Highlights:

Utilize Instagram Story Highlights to showcase important content, such as product categories, services, or behind-the-scenes glimpses. This allows visitors to your profile to quickly access and explore key aspects of your business.

8. Brand Personality:

Infuse your brand's personality into your bio. If your tone is friendly and casual, let that reflect in your language. If your brand is more formal, maintain a professional tone. Consistency in your brand voice helps create a cohesive and memorable identity.

9. Update and Evolve:

Your Instagram bio is not set in stone. Regularly revisit and update it to reflect changes in your business, promotions, or evolving brand messaging. Keeping your bio current ensures that it remains an accurate representation of your business.

10. Analytics and Testing:

Leverage Instagram Insights to analyze the performance of your bio. Track metrics such as profile visits and follower growth to understand the impact of your bio. Consider experimenting with variations to see what resonates best with your audience.

Crafting a compelling Instagram bio is an art that involves a mix of creativity, clarity, and strategic thinking. Take the time to refine and perfect your bio, ensuring it serves as a welcoming and informative entry point to your Instagram business profile. As you engage with your audience, your bio becomes a crucial tool in making a memorable and positive first impression.

- Choosing the Right Profile Picture

Your Instagram profile picture is the visual representation of your brand – the first thing users notice when they come across your profile. Making a positive and memorable impression starts with selecting the right profile picture. Here's a guide to help you choose a compelling image.

1. Brand Logo or Recognizable Image:
Opt for a brand logo or a visually distinctive image that represents your business. A recognizable logo ensures immediate association with your brand, while a unique image can convey the essence of your offerings.

2. Consistency Across Platforms:
Maintain consistency with your profile picture across all your online platforms. Whether it's Instagram, Facebook, or

Twitter, using the same or a visually similar profile picture enhances brand recognition and coherence.

3. Clear and High-Quality Image:

Ensure your profile picture is clear, high-resolution, and well-lit. A blurry or pixelated image can detract from your professionalism. Aim for a visually appealing picture that reflects the quality and standards of your brand.

4. Framing and Composition:

Focus on simplicity and effective composition. Your profile picture will appear as a small circle on Instagram, so choose an image that is easily recognizable even in this condensed format. Avoid clutter and ensure the central elements are visible.

Align your profile picture with your brand's visual aesthetics. If your brand has a specific color palette or design elements, incorporate them into the profile picture to maintain a cohesive and branded look.

6. Show Personality:

Infuse personality into your profile picture to make it more relatable. Depending on your brand tone, consider adding a touch of friendliness, professionalism, or creativity to connect with your audience on a personal level.

7. Consider Branding Elements:

If your brand uses specific branding elements, such as a mascot, tagline, or signature style, consider incorporating them into your profile picture. This adds uniqueness and reinforces brand identity.

8. Test for Recognition:

Test the recognizability of your profile picture by asking friends, colleagues, or even existing customers. If they can easily identify your brand from the profile picture alone, you've likely chosen an effective image.

9. Check Thumbnail Appearance:

Keep in mind that your profile picture will appear as a thumbnail in comments and direct messages. Test how it looks in this smaller format to ensure it remains distinct and recognizable.

10. Adapt to Changes:

While consistency is crucial, be open to updating your profile picture to reflect changes in branding, campaigns, or significant milestones. This flexibility ensures your profile picture remains relevant and aligned with your current business identity.

Choosing the right profile picture is a strategic decision that contributes to your overall brand image on Instagram. By thoughtfully considering elements like brand representation, quality, and recognizability, you set the stage for a positive and visually appealing presence that resonates with your audience.

- Optimizing Contact Information

Effective communication is a cornerstone of successful business interactions, and optimizing your contact information on your Instagram business profile is a crucial step towards enhancing accessibility. Here's a guide to help you maximize the utility of this section.

1. Business Email Address:

Include a dedicated business email address in your contact information. This provides a formal channel for inquiries, collaborations, and customer communication. A professional email address reinforces credibility and makes it easy for potential clients or customers to reach out.

2. Phone Number:

If applicable and comfortable for your business model, consider adding a business phone number. This can be especially useful for direct inquiries or customer support. Ensure that the phone number provided is actively monitored to promptly address incoming calls or messages.

3. Physical Address (if applicable):

If you have a physical location, such as a store or office, consider adding your business address. This is particularly relevant for local businesses or those with brick-and-mortar establishments. Providing an address can enhance trust and make it easier for customers to locate you.

4. Website Link:

Include a link to your business website. This serves as a gateway for users to explore more about your products, services, or brand story. Make sure the link directs users to a relevant landing page that aligns with their expectations based on your Instagram content.

5. Social Media Links:

If your business is active on other social media platforms, such as Facebook or Twitter, consider adding these links. This cross-platform visibility helps users connect with your brand on multiple fronts, reinforcing your online presence.

6. Utilize Instagram Action Buttons:

Instagram offers Action Buttons that allow users to take specific actions directly from their heir profile, such as making a reservation, booking an appointment, or ordering food. Depending on your business type, explore the available Action Buttons to streamline user engagement.

7. Highlight Contact Information in Bio:
Reiterate key contact details in your bio. While your contact information section is easily accessible, having essential details in your bio ensures that users can quickly find the information they need without navigating away from the main profile page.

8. Regularly Update Information:
Ensure that your contact information is up to date. If there are any changes to your email address, phone number, or business location, promptly update this information on your Instagram profile. Keeping details current fosters trust and reliability.

9. Use a Link in the Bio Tool:
Given that Instagram allows only one clickable link in the bio, consider using a link-in bio tool to create a landing page that aggregates multiple links. These tools enable you to direct users to various pages,

making it easier for them to access relevant information.

10. Privacy Considerations:

Be mindful of privacy concerns, especially when sharing contact information. If your business primarily operates online or does not require a physical location, focus on providing the most relevant and necessary contact details to maintain a balance between accessibility and privacy.

By optimizing your contact information on your Instagram business profile, you create a seamless pathway for potential clients, customers, and collaborators to connect with your brand. Whether through email, phone, or direct messages, fostering easy communication contributes to building strong relationships and enhancing the overall user experience.

Chapter 3.

Content Creation Strategies

- Crafting Engaging Visuals

In the visually-driven landscape of Instagram, crafting engaging visuals is a key component of a successful content creation strategy. Here are strategies to help you create compelling visuals that captivate your audience and elevate your brand presence.

1. Know Your Audience:

Understanding your target audience is fundamental to crafting visuals that resonate. Consider their preferences, interests, and the visual language that appeals to them. Tailor your visuals to evoke emotions and connect with your audience on a personal level.

2. Consistent Branding Elements:

Maintain consistency in your visuals by incorporating recognizable branding elements. This includes using consistent colors, fonts, and design elements. A cohesive visual identity strengthens brand recall and fosters a unified brand image.

3. High-Quality Imagery:

Prioritize high-quality images and visuals. Whether it's product photography, lifestyle shots, or graphics, clear and crisp visuals convey professionalism and attention to detail. Invest in good equipment and editing tools to enhance the overall quality.

4. Storytelling through Imagery:

Each visual should contribute to the overarching story of your brand. Whether telling the journey of a product, showcasing behind-the-scenes moments, or narrating a customer's experience, use visuals as a storytelling tool to engage and connect with your audience.

5. Varied Content Types:

Diversify your content by incorporating different types of visuals. Experiment with carousel posts, videos, infographics, and user-generated content. The variety keeps your content interesting and caters to different preferences within your audience.

6. Captivating Captions:

Combine engaging visuals with compelling captions. A thoughtful caption can provide context, convey a brand message, or prompt user interaction. The synergy of captivating visuals and impactful captions creates a more immersive and memorable experience.

7. Utilize Instagram Features:

Leverage Instagram's features to enhance your visuals. Explore filters, stickers, and other creative tools to add a unique touch to your content. Stay updated with new features introduced by Instagram and incorporate them into your content strategy.

8. Embrace User-Generated Content (UGC):

Encourage your audience to create content related to your brand. Sharing UGC not only builds a sense of community but also provides authentic visuals that resonate with your audience. Request permission before reposting and credit the creators.

9. Optimize for Mobile Viewing:

Since Instagram is primarily a mobile platform, ensure your visuals are optimized for mobile viewing. Pay attention to how your content appears on smaller screens and prioritize mobile-friendly designs.

10. Analyze and Iterate:

Regularly analyze the performance of your visuals using Instagram Insights. Pay attention to metrics like engagement, reach, and audience demographics. Use these insights to refine your content creation strategy and tailor visuals to what resonates best with your audience.

Crafting engaging visuals on Instagram is an art that involves a combination of creativity, strategy, and adaptability. By staying attuned to your audience, maintaining visual consistency, and experimenting with diverse content types, you can create a visually compelling Instagram presence that not only captures attention but also fosters lasting connections with your audience.

- Developing a Consistent Brand Aesthetic

In the visually vibrant world of Instagram, establishing a consistent brand aesthetic is pivotal for creating a cohesive and memorable identity. A unified visual language not only reinforces brand recognition but also enhances the overall user experience. Here's a guide to help you develop and maintain a consistent brand aesthetic on Instagram.

1. Define Your Brand Identity:
   Start by clearly defining your brand identity. Consider your brand's values, personality, and the emotions you want to evoke in your audience. These foundational elements will guide the development of your visual aesthetic.

2. Choose a Core Color Palette:

Select a cohesive color palette that aligns with your brand. Consistency in color choices contributes significantly to a recognizable brand aesthetic. Whether it's bold and vibrant or subtle and muted, let your chosen colors permeate your visuals consistently.

3. Establish Visual Elements:

Identify and establish key visual elements that represent your brand. This may include specific fonts, graphic styles, or recurring motifs. These consistent elements contribute to a cohesive look across all your content.

4. Create a Style Guide:

Develop a style guide that outlines your brand aesthetic elements. Include details such as color codes, typography guidelines, image treatments, and any other visual specifications. This guide serves as a reference for maintaining visual consistency.

5. Consistent Filters and Editing Techniques:

Choose filters and editing techniques that complement your brand aesthetic. Consistently applying these filters across your visuals creates a cohesive and polished look. Experiment with different editing styles to find the one that best aligns with your brand.

6. Align with Brand Values:

Ensure that your brand aesthetic aligns with your overall brand values and messaging. If your brand emphasizes sustainability, for example, incorporate eco-friendly visuals and tones into your aesthetic choices.

7. Curate Your Instagram Grid:

Pay attention to the overall look of your Instagram grid. Consider how individual posts complement each other when viewed together. A well-curated grid enhances the aesthetic appeal of your profile.

8. Prioritize Visual Storytelling:

Weave a narrative through your visuals. Whether it's showcasing product journeys, behind-the-scenes glimpses, or customer stories, use your brand aesthetic to tell a cohesive and compelling story.

9. Maintain Consistency Across Content Types:

Whether you're sharing images, videos, carousel posts, or stories, maintain a consistent visual style. This ensures that your brand aesthetic is recognizable across all content types and formats.

10. Evolve with Purpose:

While consistency is key, allow for evolution with purpose. As your brand grows or as trends shift, consider subtle adjustments to your aesthetic. The key is to evolve in a way that maintains overall coherence and aligns with your brand's journey.

Developing a consistent brand aesthetic on Instagram is an ongoing process that involves thoughtful planning, creative exploration, and a keen eye for detail. By adhering to your brand identity, curating a unified visual language, and adapting purposefully over time, you can create an Instagram presence that not only resonates with your audience but also stands out in the ever-evolving world of social media.

- Utilizing Instagram's Features (Stories, Reels, IGTV)

Instagram offers a variety of features that can enhance your social media presence and engagement.

1. Stories:
- Leverage Instagram Stories for ephemeral content that lasts 24 hours. Share behind-the-scenes glimpses, product launches, or daily updates to connect with your audience in real time.
- Use interactive elements like polls, questions, and quizzes to encourage user engagement and gather valuable feedback.

- Utilize the Swipe-Up feature if you have over 10k followers to direct traffic to external links, promoting products, articles, or your website.

2. Reels:
- Create short, engaging videos with Instagram Reels to showcase your creativity and capture attention quickly. Utilize music, effects, and filters to enhance your content.
- Leverage trending challenges and incorporate relevant hashtags to increase discoverability. Engage with popular trends to reach a broader audience.

3. IGTV (Instagram TV):
- IGTV allows for longer-form videos, providing an opportunity to share

in-depth content, tutorials, or interviews.

- Craft a compelling IGTV series to keep your audience coming back for more. Consistency is key in building a loyal viewership.

- Promote your IGTV videos on your main feed and Stories to maximize visibility and encourage followers to explore your longer content.

4. Consistent Branding:

- Maintain a consistent visual aesthetic across all features. This reinforces your brand identity and makes your content easily recognizable.

- Use Instagram's editing tools and filters to create a cohesive look for your Stories, Reels, and IGTV videos.

5. Analytics and Insights:

- Regularly check Instagram Insights to understand your audience demographics, engagement rates, and popular content. Adjust your strategy based on these insights to improve performance.

- Track the success of your Stories, Reels, and IGTV content separately to identify what resonates most with your audience.

By strategically utilizing Instagram's diverse features, you can not only keep your content fresh and engaging but also build a stronger connection with your followers. Experiment with different formats, stay on top of trends and analyze your data to refine your approach over time.

Chapter 4.

Building and Growing Your Audience

- Identifying Your Target Audience

Identifying your target audience is a fundamental step in creating a successful marketing strategy.

1. Define Your Product or Service:
   - Clearly understand what you are offering. Identify its unique selling points and the problems it solves. This forms the basis for determining your target audience.

2. Market Research:

- Conduct thorough market research to identify potential customers. Analyze demographics, psychographics, and behavior patterns relevant to your product or service.

3. Demographics:

- Consider factors such as age, gender, location, income, and occupation. Understanding the demographic profile of your potential customers helps tailor your messaging effectively.

4. Psychographics:

- Dive into the interests, values, attitudes, and lifestyles of your audience. This information aids in creating content and campaigns that resonate on a deeper level.

5. Behavioral Characteristics:

- Examine the buying behavior, preferences, and usage patterns related to your product. Are your customers impulse buyers, or do they conduct extensive research before making a decision?

6. Competitor Analysis:

- Study your competitors and their customer base. Identify gaps in the market and areas where you can differentiate yourself to attract a specific audience.

7. Create Buyer Personas:

- Develop detailed buyer personas that represent your ideal customers. These fictional characters embody the traits of your target audience and guide your marketing efforts.

8. Feedback and Surveys:

- Actively seek feedback from existing customers. Conduct surveys to understand their preferences and pain points. This firsthand information is invaluable for refining your target audience.

9. Utilize Analytics Tools:

- Leverage analytics tools on your website, social media, and other platforms to track user behavior. Analyzing this data provides insights into who is interacting with your brand.

10. Adapt and Refine:

- Recognize that your target audience may evolve. Regularly

reassess your strategy based on changing market trends, customer feedback, and the performance of your campaigns.

By thoroughly identifying and understanding your target audience, you can tailor your marketing efforts to effectively reach and resonate with the right people. This targeted approach not only improves your chances of conversion but also builds a more loyal customer base.

- Hashtag Strategies for Visibility

Hashtag strategies play a crucial role in enhancing visibility across social media platforms. To maximize your reach, consider these effective approaches:

1. Relevance is Key:
   Ensure your hashtags align with your content. Relevance boosts visibility among users genuinely interested in your niche.

2. Mix Popular and Niche Hashtags:
   Combine popular hashtags with niche-specific ones. This broadens your exposure while targeting a more engaged audience.

3. Create Branded Hashtags:

Develop unique hashtags associated with your brand or campaign. Encourage followers to use them, fostering a community and amplifying your reach.

4. Research Trending Hashtags:

Stay current with trending hashtags in your industry. Incorporate these into your posts to capitalize on ongoing conversations and increase visibility.

5. Optimize Hashtag Count:

Tailor the number of hashtags based on the platform. While Instagram favors multiple hashtags, Twitter and Facebook may benefit from a more restrained approach.

6. Monitor Competitors:

Analyze the hashtags your competitors use. Identify trends and incorporate relevant ones into your strategy to stay competitive in your field.

7. Location-Based Hashtags:

If your content is location-specific, include relevant location-based hashtags. This can attract local audiences and enhance visibility in specific regions.

8. Consistency is Crucial:

Establish consistency in hashtag usage across your posts. This builds recognition and makes it easier for followers to associate specific hashtags with your brand.

9. Engage in Trend Challenges:

Participate in popular challenges by using associated hashtags. This not only boosts visibility but also connects you with a broader audience participating in the trend.

10. Monitor Analytics:

Regularly analyze the performance of your hashtags. Identify which ones yield the highest engagement and adjust your strategy accordingly.

Remember, a thoughtful hashtag strategy goes beyond merely increasing visibility – it fosters engagement and cultivates a community around your brand.

- **Collaborations and Partnerships**

Collaborations and partnerships can be powerful strategies to amplify your brand, reach new audiences, and foster innovation. Here's how you can make the most of such endeavors:

1. Align with Complementary Brands:
   - Seek partnerships with brands that share similar values and target audiences. This alignment ensures a more natural and mutually beneficial collaboration.

2. Define Clear Objectives:
   - Clearly outline the goals of the collaboration. Whether it's expanding reach, co-creating products, or tapping

into each other's expertise, having defined objectives helps guide the partnership.

3. Leverage Influencers and Thought Leaders:

   - Partner with influencers or thought leaders in your industry. Their endorsement can lend credibility to your brand and expose it to a wider, engaged audience.

4. Co-Creation of Content:

   - Collaborate on creating unique and engaging content. This could include joint social media campaigns, blog posts, videos, or even exclusive products. The shared content should reflect the essence of both brands.

5. Cross-Promotions:

- Utilize cross-promotions to leverage each other's audiences. This can involve featuring each other in newsletters, sharing social media posts, or running joint promotions to encourage audience crossover.

6. Events and Sponsorships:
- Collaborate on hosting or sponsoring events. This could range from webinars and workshops to physical events. Co-branded events help both partners tap into each other's networks.

7. Customer Benefits:
- Ensure that the collaboration brings value to your customers. Whether it's exclusive discounts, access to unique products, or special events, make the

collaboration rewarding for your shared audience.

8. Communication and Transparency:

- Maintain open communication with your partner. Transparency is crucial to building trust and ensuring a successful collaboration. Clearly outline responsibilities, timelines, and expectations.

9. Measure and Analyze:

- Use analytics tools to measure the impact of the collaboration. Track key performance indicators (KPIs) such as engagement, reach, and sales to assess the success of the partnership.

10. Adapt and Learn:

- Be open to adapting your strategy based on the partnership's performance. Learn from the experience and apply those insights to future collaborations to continually refine your approach.

Collaborations and partnerships, when executed thoughtfully, can significantly elevate your brand's presence and create lasting connections with both existing and new audiences. The key lies in finding partners that complement your brand, setting clear goals, and creating mutually beneficial experiences for all involved.

Chapter 5.

Effective Engagement Techniques

- Fostering Meaningful Connections

Effective Engagement Techniques: Fostering Meaningful Connections on Instagram

In the bustling landscape of Instagram, fostering meaningful connections with your audience goes beyond likes and comments—it involves creating a genuine and interactive community.

Elevate your engagement strategies with these techniques designed to establish lasting connections and strengthen your brand's relationship with its followers.

1. Authentic Interaction:

Engage with your audience authentically. Respond to comments on your posts, direct messages, and mentions. Show genuine interest in your followers' opinions, questions, and feedback. Authenticity forms the foundation of meaningful connections.

2. Utilize Instagram Stories:

Leverage Instagram Stories to provide real-time updates, behind-the-scenes content, and interactive elements like polls and quizzes. The ephemeral nature of

Stories encourages daily engagement and fosters a more personal connection with your audience.

3. Respond to Direct Messages:

Actively respond to direct messages from your followers. Whether it's customer inquiries, collaboration proposals, or general messages, timely and thoughtful responses show that you value and prioritize your audience.

4. Host Q&A Sessions:

Conduct Q&A sessions through Instagram Live or Stories. Invite your audience to ask questions, and respond in real-time. This not only provides valuable information but also humanizes your brand by showcasing the faces behind it.

5. User-Generated Content (UGC) Campaigns:

Encourage your followers to create content related to your brand. Whether it's using a branded hashtag or participating in a challenge, sharing UGC not only showcases your community but also strengthens the sense of belonging among your audience.

6. Conduct Contests and Giveaways:

Organize contests or giveaways to incentivize engagement. Whether it's liking, commenting, or sharing your content, these initiatives not only boost visibility but also create excitement and enthusiasm within your community.

7. Feature Your Followers:

Acknowledge and appreciate your followers by featuring their content on your profile. Whether it's a customer testimonial, a product showcase, or a creative post, giving your followers a spotlight builds a sense of camaraderie and connection.

8. Engage in Industry Conversations:

Participate in conversations within your industry or niche. Engage with relevant hashtags, comment on posts from other accounts in your niche, and share your insights. This not only expands your reach but also positions your brand within a broader community.

9. Share Personal Stories:

Share personal anecdotes, team highlights, or stories that reflect your brand's values. Providing glimpses into the human side of your brand fosters a deeper connection, as followers can relate to the people behind the content.

10. Host Instagram Live Sessions:

Host live sessions to connect with your audience in real time. Whether it's a live Q&A, a product demonstration, or a discussion on relevant topics, Instagram Live allows for direct interaction, creating a sense of immediacy and connection.

11. Create Interactive Content:

Craft content that encourages interaction. Use features like polls, quizzes, and interactive stickers in your Stories to invite participation. Interactive content not only engages your audience but also provides valuable insights into their preferences.

By incorporating these engagement techniques into your Instagram strategy, you can go beyond surface-level interactions and foster genuine connections with your audience. Building a community that actively engages with and supports your brand not only strengthens loyalty but also contributes to the organic growth and sustainability of your presence on Instagram.

- Responding to Comments and DMs

Engaging with your audience on Instagram doesn't end with posting captivating content—it extends to actively responding to comments and direct messages. Cultivating these interactions is crucial for building relationships, fostering community, and demonstrating the human side of your brand. Here's a guide on how to effectively respond to comments and DMs on Instagram.

1. Timely Responses:

Aim for timely responses to comments and direct messages. A prompt acknowledgment demonstrates attentiveness and lets your audience know that their input is valued.

2. Express Gratitude:

Start your responses with expressions of gratitude. Whether it's a compliment, a question, or feedback, thanking your audience for their engagement sets a positive tone for the interaction.

3. Personalized Responses:

Personalize your responses by addressing users by their usernames. This small touch adds a human element and makes followers feel acknowledged as individuals rather than just part of a broader audience.

4. Ask Questions:

Encourage further engagement by asking questions in your responses. This invites users to share more about themselves or express their opinions, turning the interaction into a conversation.

5. Be Genuine:

Approach your responses with authenticity. Genuine and sincere interactions contribute to a positive brand image and build trust among your audience.

6. Handle Constructive Criticism Gracefully:

If faced with constructive criticism, respond gracefully. Acknowledge the feedback, express your understanding, and assure users that their opinions are valued. This demonstrates a commitment to improvement and transparency.

7. Use Emojis Mindfully:

Emojis can add a touch of personality to your responses, but use them mindfully. Ensure that emojis align with the tone of your brand and the nature of the conversation.

8. Address Concerns Privately:

If a follower raises a concern or issue in the comments, consider addressing it privately through direct messages. This allows for a more personalized and confidential resolution.

9. Set Expectations for DMs:

In your captions or Stories, set clear expectations for direct messages. If you prefer inquiries to be sent through DMs, communicate this to your audience. This can help manage expectations and streamline communication.

10. Embrace Positive Conversations:

Amplify positive conversations within the comments section. Responding to positive comments not only acknowledges and appreciates your audience but also encourages a supportive community culture.

11. Use Canned Responses for Efficiency:

For frequently asked questions or common inquiries, consider using canned responses. This ensures efficiency while maintaining a personalized touch in your interactions.

12. Keep Conversations Open-Ended:

When responding to direct messages, keep conversations open-ended. Instead of providing brief answers, encourage users to share more about their thoughts or experiences.

13. Know When to Take Offline:

For complex issues or detailed discussions, consider suggesting a transition to email or another platform. This ensures that the conversation can be adequately addressed without limitations.

Responding to comments and direct messages on Instagram is not just about communication—it's about building a community and fostering connections. By approaching interactions with attentiveness, authenticity, and a genuine interest in your audience, you contribute to a positive and engaging online environment that reflects the values of your brand.

- Running Contests and Giveaways

Contests and giveaways are potent tools on Instagram for creating buzz, fostering engagement, and expanding your reach. When executed strategically, these initiatives not only generate excitement among your audience but also contribute to brand visibility and community growth. Here's a comprehensive guide to running successful contests and giveaways on Instagram.

1. Define Your Objectives:
   Clearly outline your goals for the contest or giveaway. Whether it's increasing brand awareness, growing your follower count, promoting a new

product, or encouraging user-generated content, having specific objectives will guide your strategy.

2. Choose the Right Type of Contest:

Select a contest format that aligns with your goals and resonates with your audience. Popular options include like-to-enter, comment-to-enter, photo contests, and user-generated content challenges. Tailor the format to encourage desired interactions.

3. Set Clear Rules and Guidelines:

Communicate the rules and guidelines of your contest or giveaway. Specify the entry requirements, duration, eligibility criteria, and how winners will be selected. Transparency builds trust and ensures a smooth and fair process.

4. Leverage Compelling Prizes:

The allure of prizes is a primary motivator for participation. Offer prizes that resonate with your audience and align with your brand. Consider exclusive products, discounts, collaborations with other brands, or experiences that create genuine excitement.

5. Create Eye-Catching Visuals:

Design visually appealing and attention-grabbing graphics or images to promote your contest. Use clear and concise text to convey the details, entry instructions, and deadline. The visual presentation should be consistent with your brand aesthetic.

6. Craft a Compelling Caption:

Your contest caption is an opportunity to convey enthusiasm and encourage participation. Clearly articulate the benefits of entering, highlight the prizes, and express gratitude for your followers' engagement.

7. Utilize Hashtags Effectively:

Create a branded hashtag specifically for your contest to streamline entries and monitor engagement. Encourage participants to use the hashtag in their entries and when sharing your contest, enhancing visibility and creating a sense of community.

8. Partner with Influencers or Collaborate:

Amplify the reach of your contest by partnering with influencers or collaborating with other brands. This can extend your contest to new audiences, leveraging the influencer's following or the collaborative brand's customer base.

9. Promote Across Multiple Channels:

Extend the reach of your contest by promoting it across various channels. Share teasers on Stories, post announcements on your feed and utilize other social media platforms to create a comprehensive promotional strategy.

10. Engage with Participants:

Actively engage with participants by responding to comments, liking entries, and sharing user-generated content. This not only boosts participant morale but also creates a dynamic and supportive community around your brand.

11. Announce Winners Transparently:

When the contest concludes, announce the winners transparently. Whether through a dedicated winner announcement post or a Stories update, ensure that the process is clear, fair, and adheres to the previously communicated guidelines.

12. Follow Up with Post-Contest Content:

After the contest, continue to engage with your audience by sharing content related to the event. This could include showcasing entries, highlighting winners, or sharing behind-the-scenes glimpses. Sustain the post-contest excitement and maintain momentum.

By incorporating these strategies, your Instagram contests and giveaways can become powerful tools for fostering engagement, building excitement, and strengthening the connection between your brand and its audience. Remember that authenticity, creativity, and a genuine interest in your audience's participation are key elements of a successful contest or giveaway campaign.

Chapter 6.

Analytics and Optimization

- Utilizing Instagram Insights

Contests and giveaways are potent tools on Instagram for creating buzz, fostering engagement, and expanding your reach. When executed strategically, these initiatives not only generate excitement among your audience but also contribute to brand visibility and community growth. Here's a comprehensive guide to running successful contests and giveaways on Instagram.

1. Define Your Objectives:

Clearly outline your goals for the contest or giveaway. Whether it's increasing brand awareness, growing your follower count, promoting a new product, or encouraging user-generated content, having specific objectives will guide your strategy.

2. Choose the Right Type of Contest:

Select a contest format that aligns with your goals and resonates with your audience. Popular options include like-to-enter, comment-to-enter, photo contests, and user-generated content challenges. Tailor the format to encourage desired interactions.

3. Set Clear Rules and Guidelines:

Clearly communicate the rules and guidelines of your contest or giveaway. Specify the entry requirements, duration, eligibility criteria, and how winners will be selected. Transparency builds trust and ensures a smooth and fair process.

4. Leverage Compelling Prizes:

The allure of prizes is a primary motivator for participation. Offer prizes that resonate with your audience and align with your brand. Consider exclusive products, discounts, collaborations with other brands, or experiences that create genuine excitement.

5. Create Eye-Catching Visuals:

Design visually appealing and attention-grabbing graphics or images to promote your contest. Use clear and concise text to convey the details, entry instructions, and deadline. The visual presentation should be consistent with your brand aesthetic.

6. Craft a Compelling Caption:

Your contest caption is an opportunity to convey enthusiasm and encourage participation. Clearly articulate the benefits of entering, highlight the prizes, and express gratitude for your followers' engagement.

7. Utilize Hashtags Effectively:

Create a branded hashtag specifically for your contest to streamline entries and monitor engagement. Encourage participants to use the hashtag in their entries and when sharing your contest, enhancing visibility and creating a sense of community.

8. Partner with Influencers or Collaborate:

Amplify the reach of your contest by partnering with influencers or collaborating with other brands. This can extend your contest to new audiences, leveraging the influencer's following or the collaborative brand's customer base.

9. Promote Across Multiple Channels:

Extend the reach of your contest by promoting it across various channels. Share teasers on Stories, post announcements on your feed, and utilize other social media platforms to create a comprehensive promotional strategy.

10. Engage with Participants:

Actively engage with participants by responding to comments, liking entries, and sharing user-generated content. This not only boosts participant morale but also creates a dynamic and supportive community around your brand.

11. Announce Winners Transparently:

When the contest concludes, announce the winners transparently. Whether through a dedicated winner announcement post or a Stories update, ensure that the process is clear, fair, and adheres to the previously communicated guidelines.

12. Follow Up with Post-Contest Content:

After the contest, continue to engage with your audience by sharing content related to the event. This could include showcasing entries, highlighting winners, or sharing behind-the-scenes glimpses. Sustain the post-contest excitement and maintain momentum.

By incorporating these strategies, your Instagram contests and giveaways can become powerful tools for fostering engagement, building excitement, and strengthening the connection between your brand and its audience. Remember that authenticity, creativity, and a genuine interest in your audience's participation are key elements of a successful contest or giveaway campaign.

- Analyzing Key Metrics

Understanding and analyzing key metrics is a fundamental aspect of optimizing your Instagram strategy. By delving into the data, you gain valuable insights into the performance of your content, audience engagement, and overall brand presence. Here's a comprehensive guide on analyzing key metrics to make informed decisions and enhance your Instagram presence.

1. Instagram Insights Overview:

Instagram provides a built-in analytics tool called Instagram Insights. Accessible for business and creator accounts, Insights offers a comprehensive overview of key metrics, including reach, engagement, and follower demographics.

2. Monitor Follower Growth:

Track the growth of your follower count over time. Analyzing follower trends can help identify the effectiveness of your content strategy, marketing campaigns, and overall appeal to your target audience.

3. Engagement Metrics:

Pay attention to engagement metrics, including likes, comments, and shares. Understanding which posts resonate most with your audience helps refine your content strategy and tailor future posts for maximum engagement.

4. Reach and Impressions:
Differentiating between reach and impressions is crucial. Reach represents the unique number of accounts that have seen your content, while impressions signify the total number of views, including multiple views from the same account.

5. Explore Your Audience Demographics:
Utilize Insights to explore the demographics of your audience, including age range, gender, location, and active hours. This data guides content creation and ensures

alignment with the preferences of your target demographic.

6. Content Performance Analysis:

Evaluate the performance of individual posts and content types. Identify patterns in high-performing content, such as specific themes, formats, or posting times, and replicate successful strategies.

7. Track Hashtag Performance:

If you use branded or industry-related hashtags, track their performance. Assess the reach and engagement associated with specific hashtags to refine your hashtag strategy and increase content visibility.

8. Website Clicks and Conversion Tracking:

For business accounts with linked websites, analyze clicks and conversions. Monitoring website clicks provides insights into your audience's interest and behavior beyond the Instagram platform.

9. Analyze Stories Insights:

Instagram Stories offer a unique set of metrics, including views, interactions, and completion rates. Assessing Stories Insights allows you to refine your storytelling approach and understand the content duration that resonates best.

10. Monitor IGTV and Reels Engagement:

If you utilize IGTV or Reels, track their performance metrics. Assess view counts, likes, comments, and shares to gauge the effectiveness of your long-form or short-form video content.

11. Refine Posting Schedule:

Examine the times when your audience is most active. Insights provides data on the days and hours when your followers are online, allowing you to refine your posting schedule for optimal visibility.

12. Measure Return on Investment (ROI):

If your Instagram strategy involves advertising, measure the ROI of your campaigns. Analyze metrics related to ad performance, such as click-through rates and conversion rates, to optimize your advertising strategy.

13. Benchmark Against Competitors:

Compare your performance metrics to those of competitors or industry benchmarks. Benchmarking provides context and helps identify areas for improvement or strategies that yield successful outcomes.

14. Iterate Based on Insights:

Regularly analyze key metrics and iterate your strategy based on the insights gained. Whether it's adjusting content types, refining posting times, or experimenting with new features, data-driven decisions lead to continuous improvement.

By consistently analyzing key metrics on Instagram, you empower your brand with the knowledge needed to refine your approach, better connect with your audience, and ultimately achieve your overarching business goals. Remember that the iterative nature of analysis and adaptation is the key to staying relevant and effective in the dynamic landscape of social media.

- Adjusting Strategies for Maximum Impact

In the dynamic realm of Instagram, adaptability is a cornerstone of a successful social media strategy. To maximize impact, it's essential to analyze performance regularly and make strategic adjustments. Here's a comprehensive guide on how to tweak your strategies for maximum impact and sustained growth.

1. Regularly Assess Key Metrics:

Begin by regularly assessing key metrics through Instagram Insights. Understand how your content is performing, identify trends, and glean insights into your audience's preferences and behaviors.

2. Refine Content Based on Insights:

Use the insights gathered to refine your content strategy. Focus on creating content that resonates with your audience, emphasizing successful themes, formats, and tones while adjusting elements that may not be performing as well.

3. Experiment with Content Types:

Instagram offers various content formats, from static posts and Stories to IGTV and Reels. Experiment with different content types to diversify your strategy and discover what resonates best with your audience.

4. Optimize Posting Schedule:

Analyze your audience's active hours and adjust your posting schedule accordingly. Ensure that your content is reaching the maximum number of followers by posting when they are most likely to be online.

5. Engage with Trends and Challenges:

Stay attuned to popular trends and challenges on Instagram. Participate in relevant trends to align with current conversations and tap into broader audience engagement.

6. Leverage New Features:

Instagram frequently introduces new features and tools. Stay proactive in adopting these features, such as polls, quizzes, or interactive stickers, to keep your content fresh and engage your audience in innovative ways.

7. Optimize Hashtags:

Reevaluate your hashtag strategy based on performance metrics. Experiment with new hashtags, retire underperforming ones, and ensure that your chosen hashtags align with your content and target audience.

8. Collaborate and Partner:

Collaborate with influencers, other brands, or creators in your industry. Partnerships can introduce your brand to new audiences and bring fresh perspectives to your content, fostering cross-promotional opportunities.

9. Monitor Competitor Strategies:

Keep an eye on the strategies employed by your competitors. Analyze what works well for them and adapt insights to suit your brand's unique identity. Stay informed about industry trends and shifts.

10. Test and Iterate:

Implement A/B testing for various elements of your strategy, such as posting times, content styles, or call-to-action approaches. Iteratively refine your strategy based on what yields the best results.

11. Listen to Audience Feedback:

Actively listen to audience feedback through comments, direct messages, and engagement patterns. Address concerns, respond to queries, and use the feedback loop to understand and adapt to your audience's evolving expectations.

12. Evaluate Paid Advertising Performance:

If you invest in paid advertising, regularly evaluate the performance of your campaigns. Adjust targeting parameters, ad creatives, and budget allocation based on the data to optimize your return on investment.

13. Assess Website Traffic and Conversions:

For business accounts with linked websites, assess the impact of your Instagram efforts on website traffic and conversions. Optimize website links, landing pages, and calls-to-action to enhance user experience and drive desired actions.

14. Embrace Seasonal and Timely Content:

Tailor your content to align with seasons, holidays, or timely events. Capitalize on relevant moments to connect with your audience and inject a sense of immediacy into your strategy.

15. Stay Adaptable and Agile:

The social media landscape is ever-evolving. Stay adaptable and agile in your approach, ready to pivot your strategy based on emerging trends, algorithm changes, or shifts in user behavior.

By consistently adjusting your Instagram strategies based on data-driven insights and a keen understanding of your audience, you position your brand for maximum impact and sustained growth. Embrace adaptability as a fundamental aspect of your social media journey, and leverage the flexibility to stay ahead in the dynamic world of Instagram.